Marilyn Monroe

Terry Barber

ENTERTAINERS

Marilyn Monroe is published by
Grass Roots Press, a division of Literacy Services of Canada Ltd.

www.grassrootsbooks.net

ACKNOWLEDGEMENTS

We acknowledge the financial support of the
Government of Canada for our publishing activities. Canadä

Produced with the assistance of
the Government of Alberta through the
Alberta Multimedia Development Fund. Alberta

Editor: Dr. Pat Campbell
Image research: Dr. Pat Campbell
Book design: Lara Minja

Library and Archives Canada Cataloguing in Publication

Barber, Terry, date, author
  Marilyn Monroe / Terry Barber.

(Entertainers)

ISBN 978–1–77153–106–1 (softcover)

  1. Readers for new literates. 2. Monroe, Marilyn, 1926–1962.
3. Actresses—United States—Biography. 4. Motion picture actors and actresses—United States—Biography. 5. Biographies. I. Title.

PE1126.N43B356 2017   428.6'2   C2017–904628–4

Printed in Canada.

Contents

Marilyn Monroe sits with Ronald Reagan.
1953

The Final Act

Marilyn falls in love many times. She falls in love with powerful men. These men tell her secrets. Marilyn might share these secrets. People tell Marilyn she is in danger. Now, Marilyn is dead. Is her death murder?

The front page of the Los Angeles Times.
1962

The Final Act

Marilyn has many problems. Marilyn drinks too much. Marilyn takes drugs. Marilyn finds it hard to sleep. She tries to kill herself at least four times. Now, Marilyn is dead. Is her death suicide? The police think so.

Norma Jeane at 10 months old.

Early Years

Norma Jeane is born June 1, 1926.
Norma Jeane never knows her father.
Her mother's name is Gladys. Gladys
finds life hard. She is always sad. She
cannot care for Norma Jeane. Gladys
places her baby with foster parents.

Norma Jeane is born in Los Angeles, California.

Norma Jeane sits with her mother, Gladys.

Early Years

Gladys visits Norma Jeane every Saturday. When she visits, they talk little. Gladys never hugs or kisses Norma Jeane. But they have a few good times together. Gladys takes Norma Jeane to the beach. Norma Jeane loves the beach.

Norma Jeane's mother is mentally unstable.

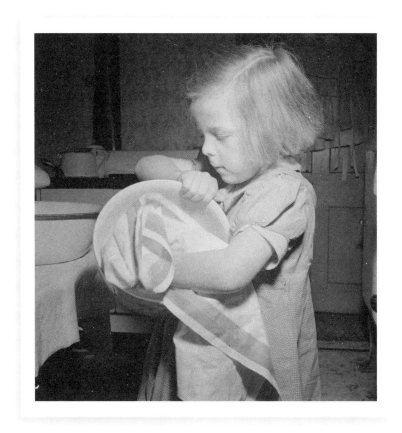

A child washes dishes.

Early Years

Norma Jeane is only a child. But her foster parents put her to work. She washes dishes. She washes clothes. She washes floors. She is told to be quiet. Norma Jeane wants a mother and father. She feels no love.

Gladys pays Norma Jeane's foster parents $5.00 a week.

Norma Jeane.
1933

Early Years

Norma Jeane loves to daydream.
She daydreams about having a father.
A father would tell her about the
world. A father would comfort her.
A father would be the best gift ever.
Norma Jeane also dreams that she will
become beautiful.

Gladys
never tells
Norma Jeane
she is pretty.

These children live at the Los Angeles orphanage.

Early Years

Gladys wants to give Norma Jeane
a good life. Gladys buys a house.
Norma Jeane moves into the house.
She is seven years old. But Gladys
cannot keep the house. Norma Jeane
is sent to the Los Angeles orphanage.

The orphanage places Norma Jeane in different foster homes.

Norma Jeane wears hand-me-down clothes.

The Outsider

School is hard for Norma Jeane. She feels like an outsider. Her clothes are old and worn. The school girls make fun of Norma Jeane. They laugh at her "orphan clothes." They call Norma Jeane dumb. But Norma Jeane knows she isn't dumb.

These children take a bus to school.

The Outsider

Norma Jeane does not have any
friends. Other girls go to parties.
Not Norma Jeane. Other girls ride the
bus to school. Norma Jeane doesn't
have a nickel to ride the bus. She is
an orphan, not like the other girls.

Norma
Jeane feels
alone and
invisible.

Jim and Norma Jeane on their wedding day.

The Outsider

When Norma Jeane turns 16, she
must make a choice. Norma Jeane
can return to the orphanage or
become a bride. Norma Jeane hates
the orphanage. She marries a man she
hardly knows. He treats her well but
Norma Jeane does not love him.

Norma
Jeane marries
Jim Dougherty on
June 19, 1942.

Marilyn (centre) models a swimsuit.

The Birth of Marilyn

In 1946, Norma Jeane gets a divorce. She changes her name to Marilyn. She wants joy in her life. Marilyn finds some joy as a model. Marilyn models for the covers of magazines. Marilyn models nude for a calendar. People begin to notice Marilyn.

Marilyn takes acting lessons at the studio.

The Birth of Marilyn

Marilyn wants to become a movie star more than anything. Marilyn knows she **lacks** talent. Many of the other actors also lack talent. But Marilyn has a desire to learn. She works hard. Marilyn has the **passion** to succeed.

Marilyn eats less to save money for acting lessons.

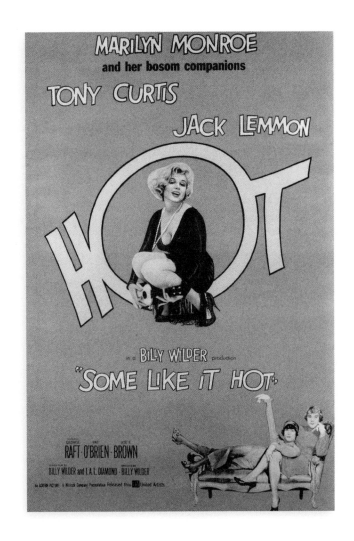

A poster for the film *Some Like it Hot*.

Stardom

Marilyn gets a movie role. Marilyn shines on the movie screen. She acts in **dramas**. One of her best films is *Some Like It Hot*. In this film, Marilyn shows her talent for comedy. Marilyn becomes one of the biggest stars in Hollywood.

Marilyn and Joe on their wedding day.

Stardom

In 1954, Marilyn marries Joe DiMaggio. Marilyn asks Joe a strange question. "When I die, will you place flowers on my grave every week?"

Joe wants Marilyn to give up her career. Their marriage lasts just nine months.

Joe DiMaggio is a famous baseball star.

Marilyn works on a movie set.

Stardom

As an actor, Marilyn is hard to work with. She arrives late on the **set**. Marilyn often forgets her lines. Marilyn gets fired more than once. But audiences love Marilyn. Audiences want to see Marilyn in more movies.

Marilyn and President Kennedy like to spend time together.

Stardom

Marilyn knows many powerful people in Hollywood. Many of these people work in politics. Marilyn meets the President. They like each other. People begin to ask questions. Is she the President's lover? Does Marilyn know too many state secrets?

The President is John F. Kennedy.

A sad little girl walks alone.

Stardom

Marilyn often feels like two people. She is Norma Jeane, the orphan. Norma Jeane belongs to nobody. She feels alone, like an outsider. She is also Marilyn Monroe, the star. Marilyn belongs to the world.

Marilyn wipes away her tears.

Stardom

In the end, fame never makes up for Marilyn's sad childhood. Fame never makes up for a childhood without love. Marilyn feels that life passes her by. She remains a little girl, more Norma Jeane than Marilyn Monroe.

Marilyn Monroe's place of rest.

Marilyn's Tragic Death

Marilyn dies on August 5, 1962. Only close friends and family attend her funeral. Others are not welcome.

Joe DiMaggio does not forget his promise. He makes sure flowers are placed on Marilyn's grave every week.

Fresh flowers show up on Marilyn's grave for 20 years.

The police search Marilyn's room after she dies.

Marilyn's Tragic Death

Marilyn's death is one of Hollywood's mysteries. People still wonder how she died. Did someone murder Marilyn? Did Marilyn kill herself with drugs and alcohol? Will we ever find out the truth? Likely not.

Marilyn's face still appears on
the front cover of magazines.

Marilyn's Tragic Death

Famous people who die young often become more famous in death. They never grow old. They keep the beauty of youth. They keep their mystery. They keep us guessing: what might have been? Marilyn Monroe is one of those people.

Glossary

drama: a movie that is about a serious subject.

lack: to be without something.

passion: a strong feeling.

set: a place where a movie or television program is filmed.

tragic: very unfortunate.

Talking About the Book

What did you learn about Marilyn Monroe?

Describe Marilyn's childhood.

As a child, what did Marilyn want?
As an adult, what did Marilyn want?

How did Marilyn's childhood affect her life as an adult?

Do you think fame fulfills Marilyn?

Do you think Marilyn's death was a murder or suicide?

Picture Credits